The
★ **UNITED** ★
STATES
PRESIDENTS

 # John

ADAMS

Heidi M.D. Elston

Big Buddy Books
An Imprint of Abdo Publishing
abdopublishing.com

abdopublishing.com

Published by Abdo Publishing, a division of ABDO, PO Box 398166, Minneapolis, Minnesota 55439.
Copyright © 2017 by Abdo Consulting Group, Inc. International copyrights reserved in all countries. No part of this book may be reproduced in any form without written permission from the publisher. Big Buddy Books™ is a trademark and logo of Abdo Publishing.

Printed in the United States of America, North Mankato, Minnesota
062016
092016

THIS BOOK CONTAINS
RECYCLED MATERIALS

Design: Sarah DeYoung, Mighty Media, Inc.
Production: Mighty Media, Inc.
Editor: Lauren Kukla
Cover Photograph: Getty Images
Interior Photographs: American Political History (p. 25); AP Images (pp. 5, 7); Corbis (pp. 6, 13);
    Getty Images (pp. 6, 7, 11, 15, 17, 23); National Park Service (p. 9); North Wind (pp. 19, 21, 27, 29)

Cataloging-in-Publication Data

Names: Elston, Heidi M.D., author.
Title: John Adams / by Heidi M.D. Elston.
Description: Minneapolis, MN : Abdo Publishing, [2017] | Series: United States
    presidents | Includes bibliographical references and index.
Identifiers: LCCN 2015957270 | ISBN 9781680780819 (lib. bdg.) |
    ISBN 9781680775013 (ebook)
Subjects: LCSH: Adams, John, 1735-1826--Juvenile literature. | Presidents
    United States--Biography--Juvenile literature. | United States--Politics and
    government--1797-1801--Juvenile literature.
Classification: DDC 973.4/4092 [B]--dc23
LC record available at http://lccn.loc.gov/2015957270

Contents

John Adams

John Adams led the fight for an independent country. He **supported** the North American colonies breaking away from Great Britain. This led to the **American Revolution**.

Adams served his country during a time of great change. He was the first US vice president. Then, he was the second US president. He did what he thought was best for Americans. Adams worked hard to bring peace to the United States.

Timeline

1735

John Adams was born in Braintree, Massachusetts, on October 30.

1775

The **American Revolution** began.

1764

On October 25, Adams married Abigail Smith.

1776

On July 4, the Continental Congress **approved** the Declaration of Independence.

1789

Adams became the nation's first vice president.

1826

On July 4, John Adams died.

1783

Adams signed the **Treaty** of Paris, which officially ended the **American Revolution**.

1797

On March 4, Adams became the second US president.

7

Early Years

John Adams was born on October 30, 1735, in Braintree, Massachusetts. His parents were John Adams and Susanna Boylston Adams. John learned to read at home. Later, he went to a local school. John soon began preparing to go to college.

★ FAST FACTS ★

Born: October 30, 1735

Wife: Abigail Smith (1744–1818)

Children: five

Political Party: Federalist

Age at Inauguration: 61

Years Served: 1797–1801

Vice President: Thomas Jefferson

Died: July 4, 1826, age 90

John's birthplace in Braintree, Massachusetts. At the time, Massachusetts was an English colony.

College and Law

In 1751, John left home to attend Harvard College. He finished school in 1755. Then, he moved to Worcester, Massachusetts. There, John began to teach. However, he soon learned he did not like teaching.

John decided to be a **lawyer** instead. He studied law for two years with a lawyer in Boston, Massachusetts. Then, in 1758, John moved back to Braintree. There, he started working as a lawyer.

At Harvard, John studied hard and earned good grades. His favorite subjects were math and science.

John and Abigail

In 1759, John met a woman named Abigail Smith. The two became close friends. In those days, most girls were not taught to read. But Abigail's parents had wanted their children to be educated. So, Abigail's mother had taught her to read.

On October 25, 1764, John and Abigail married. They had five children. Sadly, one died as a baby. Still, the Adamses were very happy. In Braintree, John farmed his land and built up his law business.

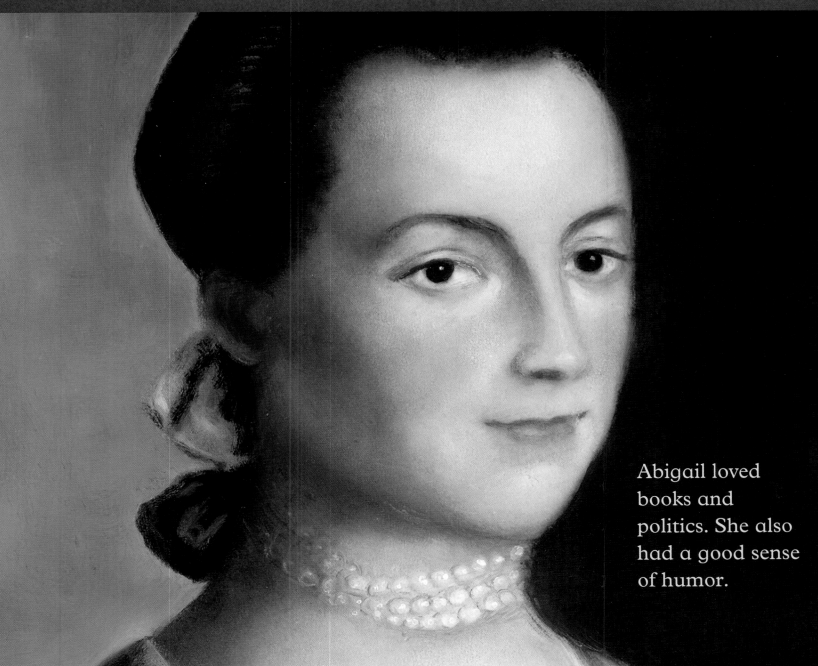

Abigail loved books and politics. She also had a good sense of humor.

Fairness for All

In 1768, the Adams family moved to Boston. There, on March 5, 1770, a fight broke out between colonists and British soldiers. The soldiers killed five colonists. This is called the Boston **Massacre**.

The soldiers went on **trial**. Adams was afraid they would not get a fair trial. So he became their **lawyer**. The colonists respected Adams because he was fair. So, he was appointed to the Massachusetts House of **Representatives**.

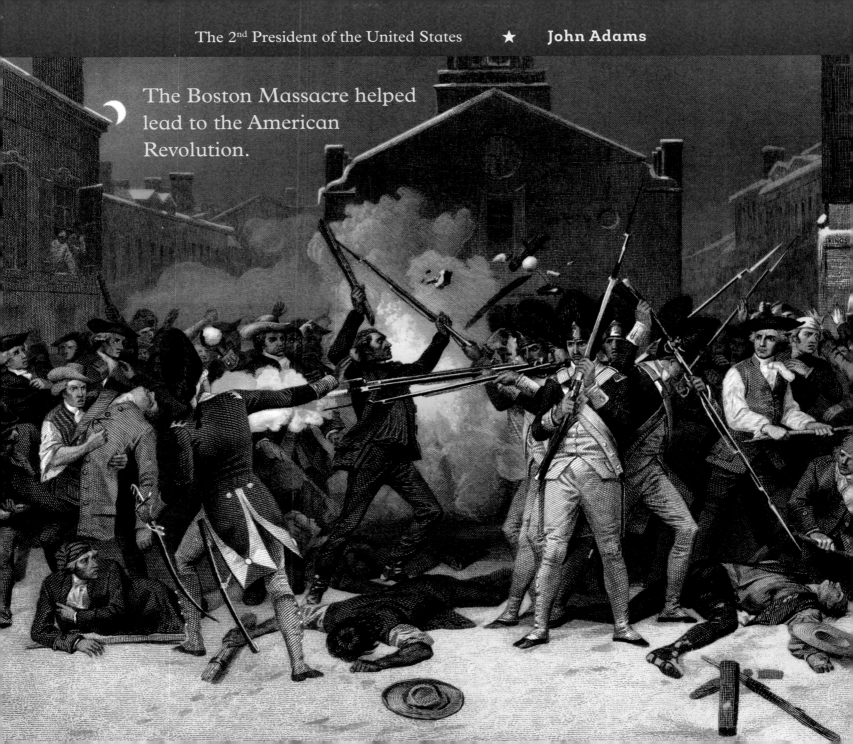

The Boston Massacre helped lead to the American Revolution.

Trouble continued between the colonists and the British. In 1773, England passed a tax on tea shipped to the colonies. But colonists **protested** the tax.

One year later, Adams attended a meeting in Pennsylvania. The **delegates** made up the First Continental Congress. Most delegates there wanted the colonies to form their own country.

The Second Continental Congress met in 1775. There, Adams helped **organize** the Continental army. He also **nominated** George Washington as its leader. The **American Revolution** had begun.

To protest the tea tax, about 60 colonists participated in the Boston Tea Party. They threw 342 chests filled with tea into Boston Harbor.

A New Nation

By 1776, the Continental Congress agreed to break from England. Adams and a few others wrote a paper. It said why the colonies should be free and independent.

On July 4, 1776, the Continental Congress **approved** the Declaration of Independence. The United States of America was born.

Adams remained a leader in the new nation. He created the American navy. Then, from 1778 to 1779, Adams spent time in France. He wanted the French to help the Americans in the war.

The Declaration of Independence was written by Thomas Jefferson, John Adams, Benjamin Franklin, Roger Sherman, and Robert R. Livingston.

In 1783, the **Treaty** of Paris was signed in France. Adams was one of the signers. The treaty officially ended the **American Revolution**.

By 1788, most states had **approved** the US **Constitution**. It named a new US Congress as head of the **federal** government. In 1789, Congress voted for the first US president.

George Washington earned the most votes. So, he became president. Adams had the second-highest number of votes. So, he became vice president.

★ DID YOU KNOW? ★

Adams was the first US president to have a son who became president.

Washington took office on April 30, 1789, in New York City.

President Adams

Adams remained vice president under Washington in the 1792 election. Then, in 1796, Adams ran for president against Thomas Jefferson. Adams won! Jefferson became his vice president.

At this time there was a **revolution** in France. Many French people were fighting their government. Jefferson wanted to help the French people. But, Adams chose to make peace with the French government. His decision angered Jefferson and members of Congress.

PRESIDENT ADAMS'S CABINET

March 4, 1797–March 4, 1801

★ **STATE:** Timothy Pickering,
John Marshall (from June 6, 1800)

★ **TREASURY:** Oliver Wolcott Jr.,
Samuel Dexter (from January 1, 1801)

★ **WAR:** James McHenry,
Samuel Dexter (from June 12, 1800)

★ **NAVY:** Benjamin Stoddert (from June 18, 1798)

★ **ATTORNEY GENERAL:** Charles Lee

In 1798, Congress passed the Alien and Sedition Acts. The Alien Acts allowed the president to **deport** people who were **foreigners**. The Sedition Act made it a crime to say bad things about the US government and its leaders.

President Adams signed both acts. But many people were against them. Adams soon realized the acts were a mistake. Adams and Jefferson ran against each other again in the 1800 election. This time, Jefferson won.

★ SUPREME COURT APPOINTMENTS ★

Bushrod Washington: 1799

Alfred Moore: 1800

John Marshall: 1801

Adams was the first president to live in the presidential mansion, now called the White House, in Washington, DC.

Return to Quincy

Adams was hurt and sad when he lost the election. He left Washington, DC, without saying good-bye to Jefferson. Mr. and Mrs. Adams went home to Braintree, now called Quincy. There, Adams wrote many letters and articles.

In 1812, Adams decided to write Jefferson. They had been good friends when they were younger. He wanted to **renew** their friendship. The letter worked! For the rest of their lives, Adams and Jefferson wrote letters to one another.

Over the years, Mr. and Mrs. Adams spent much time apart. They used letters to stay in touch.

On October 28, 1818, Abigail Adams died. Adams was very sad. Then, in 1825, Adams's son John Quincy became president. But, Adams did not get to see his son act as president for long. John Adams died on July 4, 1826.

Adams is remembered for his great **contributions** to US history. He **supported** freedom for the colonies. He helped write the Declaration of Independence. Above all, John Adams **promoted** peace for his new country.

★ DID YOU KNOW? ★

Abigail Adams was the first woman in US history to be both the wife of one president and the mother of another president.

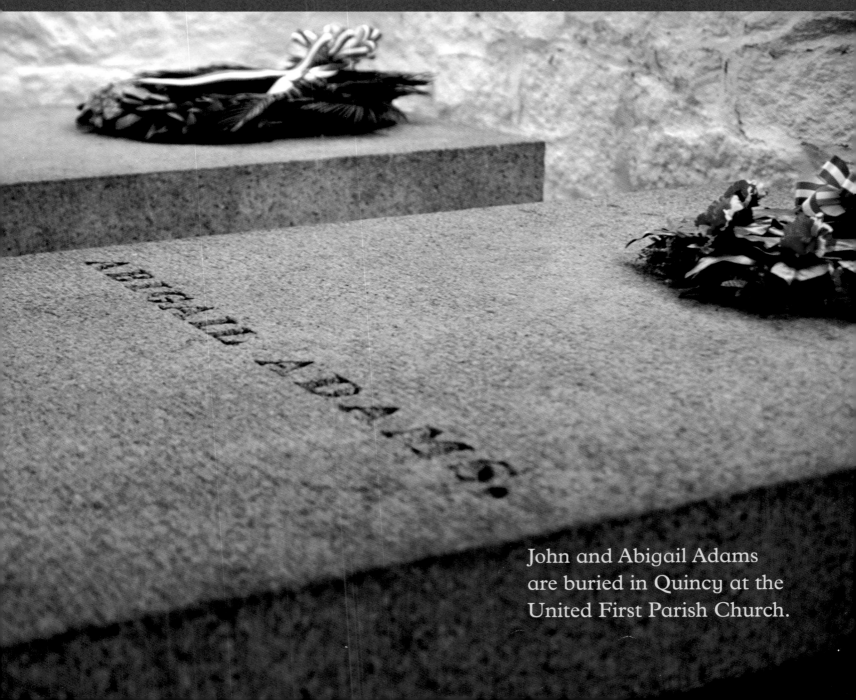

John and Abigail Adams
are buried in Quincy at the
United First Parish Church.

Office of the President

Branches of Government

The US government has three branches. They are the executive, legislative, and judicial branches. Each branch has some power over the others. This is called a system of checks and balances.

★ **Executive Branch**

The executive branch enforces laws. It is made up of the president, the vice president, and the president's cabinet. The president represents the United States around the world. He or she also signs bills into law and leads the military.

★ **Legislative Branch**

The legislative branch makes laws, maintains the military, and regulates trade. It also has the power to declare war. This branch includes the Senate and the House of Representatives. Together, these two houses form Congress.

★ **Judicial Branch**

The judicial branch interprets laws. It is made up of district courts, courts of appeals, and the Supreme Court. District courts try cases. Sometimes people disagree with a trial's outcome. Then he or she may appeal. If a court of appeals supports the ruling, a person may appeal to the Supreme Court.

Qualifications for Office

To be president, a candidate must be at least 35 years old. The person must be a natural-born US citizen. He or she must also have lived in the United States for at least 14 years.

Electoral College

The US presidential election is an indirect election. Voters from each state choose electors. These electors represent their state in the Electoral College. Each elector has one electoral vote. Electors cast their vote for the candidate with the highest number of votes from people in their state. A candidate must receive the majority of Electoral College votes to win.

Term of Office

Each president may be elected to two four-year terms. The presidential election is held on the Tuesday after the first Monday in November. The president is sworn in on January 20 of the following year. At that time, he or she takes the oath of office.
It states:

> I do solemnly swear (or affirm) that I will faithfully execute the office of President of the United States, and will to the best of my ability, preserve, protect and defend the Constitution of the United States.

Line of Succession

The Presidential Succession Act of 1947 states who becomes president if the president cannot serve. The vice president is first in the line. Next are the Speaker of the House and the President Pro Tempore of the Senate. It may happen that none of these individuals is able to serve. Then the office falls to the president's cabinet members. They would take office in the order in which each department was created:

Secretary of State

Secretary of the Treasury

Secretary of Defense

Attorney General

Secretary of the Interior

Secretary of Agriculture

Secretary of Commerce

Secretary of Labor

Secretary of Health and Human Services

Secretary of Housing and Urban Development

Secretary of Transportation

Secretary of Energy

Secretary of Education

Secretary of Veterans Affairs

Secretary of Homeland Security

Benefits

★ While in office, the president receives a salary. It is $400,000 per year. He or she lives in the White House. The president also has 24-hour Secret Service protection.

★ The president may travel on a Boeing 747 jet. This special jet is called Air Force One. It can hold 70 passengers. It has kitchens, a dining room, sleeping areas, and more. Air Force One can fly halfway around the world before needing to refuel. It can even refuel in flight!

★ When the president travels by car, he or she uses Cadillac One. It is a Cadillac Deville that has been modified. The car has heavy armor and communications systems. The president may even take Cadillac One along when visiting other countries.

★ The president also travels on a helicopter. It is called Marine One. It may also be taken along when the president visits other countries.

★ Sometimes the president needs to get away with family and friends. Camp David is the official presidential retreat. It is located in Maryland. The US Navy maintains the retreat. The US Marine Corps keeps it secure. The camp offers swimming, tennis, golf, and hiking.

★ When the president leaves office, he or she receives lifetime Secret Service protection. He or she also receives a yearly pension of $203,700. The former president also receives money for office space, supplies, and staff.

PRESIDENTS AND THEIR TERMS

PRESIDENT	PARTY	TOOK OFFICE	LEFT OFFICE	TERMS SERVED	VICE PRESIDENT
George Washington	None	April 30, 1789	March 4, 1797	Two	John Adams
John Adams	Federalist	March 4, 1797	March 4, 1801	One	Thomas Jefferson
Thomas Jefferson	Democratic-Republican	March 4, 1801	March 4, 1809	Two	Aaron Burr, George Clinton
James Madison	Democratic-Republican	March 4, 1809	March 4, 1817	Two	George Clinton, Elbridge Gerry
James Monroe	Democratic-Republican	March 4, 1817	March 4, 1825	Two	Daniel D. Tompkins
John Quincy Adams	Democratic-Republican	March 4, 1825	March 4, 1829	One	John C. Calhoun
Andrew Jackson	Democrat	March 4, 1829	March 4, 1837	Two	John C. Calhoun, Martin Van Buren
Martin Van Buren	Democrat	March 4, 1837	March 4, 1841	One	Richard M. Johnson
William H. Harrison	Whig	March 4, 1841	April 4, 1841	Died During First Term	John Tyler
John Tyler	Whig	April 6, 1841	March 4, 1845	Completed Harrison's Term	Office Vacant
James K. Polk	Democrat	March 4, 1845	March 4, 1849	One	George M. Dallas
Zachary Taylor	Whig	March 5, 1849	July 9, 1850	Died During First Term	Millard Fillmore

PRESIDENT	PARTY	TOOK OFFICE	LEFT OFFICE	TERMS SERVED	VICE PRESIDENT
Millard Fillmore	Whig	July 10, 1850	March 4, 1853	Completed Taylor's Term	Office Vacant
Franklin Pierce	Democrat	March 4, 1853	March 4, 1857	One	William R.D. King
James Buchanan	Democrat	March 4, 1857	March 4, 1861	One	John C. Breckinridge
Abraham Lincoln	Republican	March 4, 1861	April 15, 1865	Served One Term, Died During Second Term	Hannibal Hamlin, Andrew Johnson
Andrew Johnson	Democrat	April 15, 1865	March 4, 1869	Completed Lincoln's Second Term	Office Vacant
Ulysses S. Grant	Republican	March 4, 1869	March 4, 1877	Two	Schuyler Colfax, Henry Wilson
Rutherford B. Hayes	Republican	March 3, 1877	March 4, 1881	One	William A. Wheeler
James A. Garfield	Republican	March 4, 1881	September 19, 1881	Died During First Term	Chester Arthur
Chester Arthur	Republican	September 20, 1881	March 4, 1885	Completed Garfield's Term	Office Vacant
Grover Cleveland	Democrat	March 4, 1885	March 4, 1889	One	Thomas A. Hendricks
Benjamin Harrison	Republican	March 4, 1889	March 4, 1893	One	Levi P. Morton
Grover Cleveland	Democrat	March 4, 1893	March 4, 1897	One	Adlai E. Stevenson
William McKinley	Republican	March 4, 1897	September 14, 1901	Served One Term, Died During Second Term	Garret A. Hobart, Theodore Roosevelt

PRESIDENT	PARTY	TOOK OFFICE	LEFT OFFICE	TERMS SERVED	VICE PRESIDENT
Theodore Roosevelt	Republican	September 14, 1901	March 4, 1909	Completed McKinley's Second Term, Served One Term	Office Vacant, Charles Fairbanks
William Taft	Republican	March 4, 1909	March 4, 1913	One	James S. Sherman
Woodrow Wilson	Democrat	March 4, 1913	March 4, 1921	Two	Thomas R. Marshall
Warren G. Harding	Republican	March 4, 1921	August 2, 1923	Died During First Term	Calvin Coolidge
Calvin Coolidge	Republican	August 3, 1923	March 4, 1929	Completed Harding's Term, Served One Term	Office Vacant, Charles Dawes
Herbert Hoover	Republican	March 4, 1929	March 4, 1933	One	Charles Curtis
Franklin D. Roosevelt	Democrat	March 4, 1933	April 12, 1945	Served Three Terms, Died During Fourth Term	John Nance Garner, Henry A. Wallace, Harry S. Truman
Harry S. Truman	Democrat	April 12, 1945	January 20, 1953	Completed Roosevelt's Fourth Term, Served One Term	Office Vacant, Alben Barkley
Dwight D. Eisenhower	Republican	January 20, 1953	January 20, 1961	Two	Richard Nixon
John F. Kennedy	Democrat	January 20, 1961	November 22, 1963	Died During First Term	Lyndon B. Johnson
Lyndon B. Johnson	Democrat	November 22, 1963	January 20, 1969	Completed Kennedy's Term, Served One Term	Office Vacant, Hubert H. Humphrey
Richard Nixon	Republican	January 20, 1969	August 9, 1974	Completed First Term, Resigned During Second Term	Spiro T. Agnew, Gerald Ford

PRESIDENT	PARTY	TOOK OFFICE	LEFT OFFICE	TERMS SERVED	VICE PRESIDENT
Gerald Ford	Republican	August 9, 1974	January 20, 1977	Completed Nixon's Second Term	Nelson A. Rockefeller
Jimmy Carter	Democrat	January 20, 1977	January 20, 1981	One	Walter Mondale
Ronald Reagan	Republican	January 20, 1981	January 20, 1989	Two	George H.W. Bush
George H.W. Bush	Republican	January 20, 1989	January 20, 1993	One	Dan Quayle
Bill Clinton	Democrat	January 20, 1993	January 20, 2001	Two	Al Gore
George W. Bush	Republican	January 20, 2001	January 20, 2009	Two	Dick Cheney
Barack Obama	Democrat	January 20, 2009	January 20, 2017	Two	Joe Biden

"**A government of laws and not of men.**" John Adams

★ WRITE TO THE PRESIDENT ★

You may write to the president at:
The White House
1600 Pennsylvania Avenue NW
Washington, DC 20500

You may e-mail the president at:
comments@whitehouse.gov

37

Glossary

American Revolution—the war between Americans and the British from 1775 to 1783. The Americans won their freedom from the British.

approve—to officially accept something.

Constitution (kahnt-stuh-TOO-shuhn)—the basic laws that govern a country or a state.

contribution (kahn-truh-BYOO-shuhn)—the act of giving help to accomplish a goal.

delegate—someone who represents other people at a meeting or in a lawmaking group.

deport—to force someone who is not a citizen to leave the country.

federal—of or relating to the central government of the United States.

foreigner—someone from another country.

lawyer (LAW-yuhr)—a person who gives people advice on laws or represents them in court.

massacre—the murdering of many people.

nominate—to name as a possible winner.

organize—to arrange or plan something.

promote—to help something become known.

protest—to speak out against or object to something.

renew—to make new or fresh again.

Representative—someone chosen in an election to act or speak for the people who voted for him or her.

revolution—the forced overthrow of a government for a new system.

support—to believe in or be in favor of something.

treaty—an agreement made between two or more groups.

trial—the hearing and judgment of a case in a courtroom or house of Congress.

★ WEBSITES ★

To learn more about the US Presidents, visit **booklinks.abdopublishing.com**. These links are routinely monitored and updated to provide the most current information available.

Index